II TIMOTHY

STANDING FIRM IN TRUTH

• •

John Stott with
Lin Johnson

8 Studies with Commentary
for Individuals or Groups

JOHN STOTT
☩ *Bible Studies*

InterVarsity Press
Downers Grove, Illinois, USA
Leicester, UK

InterVarsity Press
P.O. Box 1400, Downers Grove, IL 60515
World Wide Web: www.ivpress.com
E-mail: mail@ivpress.com

Inter-Varsity Press
38 De Montfort Street
Leicester LE1 7GP
UK

This study guide is based on and includes excerpts adapted from The Message of 2 Timothy ©1973 by John R. W. Stott, originally published under the title Guard the Gospel.

Cover illustration: Roberta Polfus

USA ISBN 0-8308-2038-8
UK ISBN 0-85111-397-4

Printed in the United States of America ♾

19	18	17	16	15	14	13	12	11	10	9	8	7	6	5	4	3	2	1
14	13	12	11	10	09	08	07	06	05	04	03	02	01	00	99	98		

Introducing 2 Timothy

In this second imprisonment, Paul was not enjoying the comparative freedom and comfort of his own hired house in which Luke took leave of him at the end of the book of Acts and from which he seemed to have been set free as he expected. Instead, he was incarcerated in some "dismal underground dungeon with a hole in the ceiling for light and air" (William Hendrikson, *The Epistles to Timothy and Titus* [Baker Book House, 1957], p. 234). Perhaps it was the Mamertine prison, as tradition says. But wherever he was, Onesiphorus succeeded in finding him only after a painstaking search (1:17).

The preliminary hearing of Paul's case had already taken place, and he was awaiting the full trial but not expecting to be acquitted. His own apostolic labors were over. "I have finished the race," he could say. But he still had a lot on his mind and heart. Although this letter was an intensely personal communication to his young friend Timothy, it was also—and consciously—his last will and testament to the church.

Getting to Know Timothy

For over fifteen years Timothy had been Paul's faithful missionary companion. Not only did Paul have a strong affection for Timothy as a friend whom he had evidently led to Christ, had also grown to trust Timothy as his "fellow-worker" (Romans 16:21).

When the first imprisonment was over, Paul left Timothy in Ephesus as a kind of "bishop." Wide responsibilities were given to him. And now still heavier burdens were about to fall on Timothy's shoulders. For Paul was on the point of martyrdom, and then the task of preserving the apostle's teaching intact would be his in yet greater measure. Yet, humanly speaking, Timothy was hopelessly unfit to assume these weighty responsibilities.

Timothy was a real human being like us, with all the infirmity and vulnerability which that entails. To begin with, he was still comparatively young when Paul addressed this letter to him (4:12)—in his midthirties, which was still within the limits of "youth." Second, he was temperamentally shy, needing affirmation, encouragement and reassurance (2 Timothy 1:7). Third, Timothy was physically infirm and suffered from a recurrent stomach problem (5:23).

Greatness was being thrust on Timothy, and like Moses and Jeremiah and a host of others before and after him, Timothy was exceedingly reluctant to accept it.

A Message for Us
The church of our day urgently needs to heed the message of this second letter of Paul to Timothy. For all around us we see Christians relaxing their grasp of the gospel, fumbling it, in danger of letting it drop from their hands altogether. We, like Timothy, need to guard the truth of the gospel and proclaim it to the world around us.

Suggestions for Individual Study
1. As you begin each study, pray that God will speak to you through his Word.

2. Read the introduction to the study and respond to the question that follows it. This is designed to help you get into the theme of the study.

3. The studies are written in an inductive format designed to help you discover for yourself what Scripture is saying. Each study deals with a particular passage so that you can really delve into the author's meaning in that context. Read and reread the passage to be studied. The questions are written using the language of the New International Version, so you may wish to use that version of the Bible. The New Revised Standard Version is also recommended.

4. Each study includes three types of questions. *Observation* ques-

tions ask about the basic facts: who, what, when, where and how. *Interpretation* questions delve into the meaning of the passage. *Application* questions (also found in the "Apply" section) help you discover the implications of the text for growing in Christ. These three keys unlock the treasures of Scripture.

Write your answers to the study questions in the spaces provided or in a personal journal. Writing can bring clarity and deeper understanding of yourself and of God's Word.

5. In the studies you will find some commentary notes designed to give help with complex verses by giving further biblical and cultural background and contextual information. The notes in the studies are not designed to answer the questions for you. They are to help you along as you learn to study the Bible for yourself. After you have worked through the questions and notes in the guide, you may want to read the accompanying commentary by John Stott in the Bible Speaks Today series. This will give you more information about the text.

6. Move to the "Apply" section. These questions will help you connect the key biblical themes to your own life. Putting the application into practice is one of the keys to growing in Christ.

7. Use the guidelines in the "Pray" section to focus on God, thanking him for what you have learned and praying about the applications that have come to mind.

Suggestions for Members of a Group Study

1. Come to the study prepared. Follow the suggestions for individual study mentioned above. You will find that careful preparation will greatly enrich your time spent in group discussion.

2. Be willing to participate in the discussion. The leader of your group will not be lecturing. Instead, she or he will be encouraging the members of the group to discuss what they have learned. The leader will be asking the questions that are found in this guide.

3. Stick to the topic being discussed. Your answers should be based on the verses which are the focus of the discussion and not on outside authorities such as commentaries or speakers. These studies focus on a particular passage of Scripture. Only rarely should you refer to other portions of the Bible. This allows for everyone to participate on equal ground and for in-depth study.

4. Be sensitive to the other members of the group. Listen attentively when they describe what they have learned. You may be surprised by their insights! Each question assumes a variety of answers. Many questions do not have "right" answers, particularly questions that aim at meaning or application. Instead the questions push us to explore the passage more thoroughly.

When possible, link what you say to the comments of others. Also, be affirming whenever you can. This will encourage some of the more hesitant members of the group to participate.

5. Be careful not to dominate the discussion. We are sometimes so eager to express our thoughts that we leave too little opportunity for others to respond. By all means participate! But allow others to also.

6. Expect God to teach you through the passage being discussed and through the other members of the group. Pray that you will have an enjoyable and profitable time together, but also that as a result of the study you will find ways that you can take action individually and/or as a group.

7. It will be helpful for groups to follow a few basic guidelines. These guidelines, which you may wish to adapt to your situation, should be read at the beginning of the first session.

☐ Anything said in the group is considered confidential and will not be discussed outside the group unless specific permission is given to do so.

☐ We will provide time for each person present to talk if he or she feels comfortable doing so.

☐ We will talk about ourselves and our own situations, avoiding conversation about other people.

☐ We will listen attentively to each other.

☐ We will be very cautious about giving advice.

8. If you are the group leader, you will find additional suggestions at the back of the guide.

1
STAND UP
FOR THE GOSPEL

2 Timothy 1:1-10

*D*eath is the great unmentionable in our world. It is up to the church to recover its lost certainty about the victory of Jesus Christ and to declare this good news to the world.

Of course, death can be very unpleasant, and bereavement can bring bitter sorrow. But death itself has been overthrown, and "blessed are the dead who die in the Lord" (Revelation 14:13).

As the apostle Paul was languishing in some dark, dank dungeon in Rome, from which there was to be no escape but death, his thoughts turned to what it means to die in Christ. He was in chains, suffering acutely from the loneliness, boredom and cold of prison life. Is it not truly wonderful that, although Paul's body is confined within the narrow limits of an underground cell, his heart and mind can thus soar into eternity?

Open ————————————————————————

■ If you knew you were going to die in a month, how would you spend your remaining time on earth? What would occupy your mind?

Study

■ *Read 2 Timothy 1:1-7.* In this opening paragraph, we are introduced in a very vivid way to both Paul and Timothy, the writer and recipient of the letter. In particular, we are told something of how each man had come to be what he was. These verses throw light on the providence of God, on how God fashions us into what he wants us to be.

---

1. What do we learn about Paul from these opening verses?

According to verse 1, Paul had been commissioned as an apostle first to formulate and then to communicate the gospel. And the gospel is good news for dying sinners that God has promised them life in Jesus Christ. It seems particularly appropriate that, as death stares the apostle in the face, he should here define it as a "promise of life." For this is what it is. The gospel offers life—true life, eternal life—both here and hereafter.

---

2. Even though Paul was close to dying, what was on his mind when he wrote this letter? Why?

---

3. What is attractive about the relationship between Paul and Timothy?

4. What do we learn about using the gifts God has given us from Paul's reminder to Timothy in verse 6?

5. How could practicing verse 7 strengthen Timothy for his ministry?

6. How might Timothy's characteristics have been assets for or handicaps to effective ministry?

Summary: The first seven verses of the letter tell us about Paul and Timothy and their making. Paul claimed to be Jesus Christ's apostle "by the will of God." Previously he had said it was "by the grace of God" that he was what he was (1 Corinthians 15:10). And a whole complex of factors had made Timothy what he was—a godly upbringing, Paul's friendship and training, God's gift to him, and his own self-discipline in stirring it up.

In principle, it is the same with all God's people. Perhaps the most striking thing is the combination in both Paul and Timothy of divine sovereignty and human responsibility, those two facts of revelation and experience that we find difficult to reconcile and impossible to systematize into a tidy doctrine.

7. *Read 1 Timothy 1:8-10.* Paul then turned from the varied factors which had contributed to the making of Timothy to the truth of the gospel and Timothy's responsibility in relation to it. Why did Paul give Timothy the command in verse 8?

These are still the three main ways in which Christian people, like Timothy, are tempted to feel ashamed: the *name* of Christ, to whom we are called to witness; the *people* of Christ, to whom we also belong if we belong to him; and the *gospel* of Christ, which is entrusted to us to spread.

8. In what ways are we ashamed of Christ's name, other believers or the gospel?

9. In verses 9 and 10 Paul sketches out some of the main features of the gospel of which Timothy was not to be ashamed and for which he must take his share of suffering. What key words and phrases describe this gospel?

10. How can you use verses 9 and 10 to tell someone about God's salvation?

Summary: The sweep of God's purpose of grace is majestic indeed, as Paul traced it from a past eternity through a historical outworking in Jesus Christ and in the Christian to an ultimate destiny with Christ and like Christ in a future immortality.

Apply ————————————————————————————

■ Timothy was influenced spiritually by his grandmother, mother and Paul. Who can you influence in similar ways?

What will you do this week to begin or strengthen your impact?

How can you practice the truth of verse 7 to help you tell others about the gospel and to guard against being ashamed of it?

Pray

■ If you have failed to speak out for the Lord recently, ask God for forgiveness. Also ask him to help you not to be ashamed to testify about him or to be ashamed of other believers.

2
BATTLING
FOR THE TRUTH

2 Timothy 1:11-18

For thirty years or so, Paul had faithfully preached the good news, planted churches, defended the truth and consolidated the work. But what would happen to the gospel when he was dead and gone? The emperor Nero, bent on suppressing all secret societies and misunderstanding the nature of the Christian church, seemed determined to destroy it. Heretics appeared to be on the increase. There had recently been an almost total Asian apostasy from Paul's teaching. Bishop Moule goes so far as to write that "Christianity . . . trembled, *humanly speaking,* on the verge of annihilation" (*The Second Epistle to Timothy* [Religious Tract Society, 1905], p. 18). Who, then, would do battle for the truth when Paul had laid down his life? This was the question that dominated and vexed his mind as he lay in chains and which he addressed in this letter.

The apostle's appeal was urgent. He reminded Timothy that the precious gospel was now committed to *him*, and that it was now *his* turn to assume responsibility for it.

Open ——————————————————————————
■ How has your response to the gospel matured since you first heard it?

Study

■ *Read 2 Timothy 1:11-14.* Even at the end of his life, Paul focused on the gospel. If we were to ask him what our first duty is in relation to the gospel, he would of course say to receive it and live by it. But his concern here is not with the unbeliever's duty but with the duty of Christians toward the gospel after they have embraced it.

1. What words and phrases throughout these verses indicate the tone of Paul's message?

2. Paul defines himself in three specific roles in verse 11. What is the significance of each?

3. How are the roles Paul mentions in verse 11 the cause of his suffering (v. 12)?

4. What motivated Paul to endure such suffering as imprisonment?

5. How can Paul's motivation encourage you when it's difficult to be a Christian?

---

6. In addition to not being ashamed of the gospel, Paul outlined Timothy's responsibility in relation to it. What was that responsibility?

"Sound teaching" is healthy teaching. The Greek expression was used in the Gospels of people whom Jesus healed. Previously they had been maimed or diseased; now they were well or whole. So the Christian faith is the "sound teaching" because it is not maimed or diseased but whole. It is what Paul had previously called "the whole will of God" (Acts 20:27).

The apostolic faith is not only a standard of "sound teaching," it is also "the good deposit." The gospel is a treasure—a good, noble and precious treasure—deposited for safe-keeping with the church. Christ had entrusted it to Paul, and Paul then entrusted it to Timothy.

---

7. How could Paul's attitude in his situation encourage Timothy to keep these commands?

Summary: There is great encouragement here. Ultimately, it is God himself who is the guarantor of the gospel. It is his responsibility to preserve it. Even though it is spoken against, ridiculed and abandoned, God will never allow the light of the gospel to be finally extinguished. True, he has committed it to us, frail and fallible creatures. And we must play our part in guarding and defending the truth. Nevertheless, in entrusting the deposit to our hands, he has not taken his own hands off it. He is himself its final guardian, and *he* will preserve the truth which he has committed to the church. We know this because we know him in whom we have trusted and continue to trust.

Timothy was to guard the gospel all the more tenaciously because of what had happened in and around Ephesus (the capital of the Roman province of Asia) where Timothy was.

---

8. *Read 2 Timothy 1:15-18.* In what ways did Paul's Asian friends react to his imprisonment?

Why do you think there was such a difference in how people responded?

---

9. What examples do you see today of people like these?

Summary: The gospel is the good news of salvation, promised from eternity, secured by Christ in time, offered to faith. Our first duty is to *communicate* this gospel, to use old ways and seek fresh ways of making it known throughout the whole world. If we do so, we shall undoubtedly *suffer* for it, for the authentic gospel has never been popular. It humbles the sinner too much. And when we are called to suffer for the gospel, we are tempted to trim it, to eliminate those elements which give offense and cause opposition, to mute the notes which jar sensitive contemporary ears.

But we must resist the temptation. For, above all, we are called to *guard* the gospel, keeping it pure whatever the cost, and preserving it against every corruption. Guard it faithfully. Spread it actively. Suffer for it bravely. This is our threefold duty in relation to the gospel.

Apply

■ How can we "guard the good deposit" of the gospel today?

How can you follow Onesiphorus's example this week?

Pray

■ Ask God to help you guard the truth of the gospel and remain loyal to those who are suffering for it.

3
NO PAIN, NO GAIN

2 Timothy 2:1-13

*T*he first chapter ended with Paul's sorrowful reference to the widespread defection among Christians in the Roman province of Asia. Onesiphorus and his household seemed to have been the outstanding exception. So Paul urged Timothy that he, too, in the midst of the general landslide, must stand his ground. Timothy had been called to responsible leadership in the church, not only in spite of his natural timidity but in the very area where the apostle's authority was being challenged. It is as if Paul said to him: "Never mind what other people may be thinking or saying or doing. Never mind how weak and shy you yourself may feel. As for you, Timothy, be strong!" That same command applies to us today.

Open
■ When is it hardest for you to be strong for the Lord? Why?

Study
■ *Read 2 Timothy 2:1-2.* Paul proceeded to indicate the kind of ministry for which Timothy would need to strengthen himself. So far he had been exhorted to hold the faith and guard the deposit (1:13-14). But he was to

do more than preserve the truth, however; he was also to pass it on.

1. What key instruction is Paul giving Timothy?

2. Why did Paul tell Timothy to be strong in "grace," rather than in something else like knowledge?

3. Being strong in grace will help Timothy pass on the gospel to others. How is the process of passing on the gospel that Paul described here effective?

Read 2 Timothy 2:3-7. In the rest of this second chapter, Paul enlarged on the teaching ministry to which Timothy had been called. He illustrated it by using six vivid metaphors. The first three were favorite images with Paul; he made use of them several times in former letters to enforce a wide variety of truths.

4. The first metaphor is that of a soldier. Paul's prison experiences had given him ample opportunity to watch Roman soldiers and to meditate on the parallels between the soldier and the Christian. How does a believer "endure hardship" as a soldier?

5. What did Paul mean by cautioning against getting involved in civilian affairs?

6. Paul then turned to the image of the competitor in the Greek games. How does being an athlete relate to being a Christian?

7. The third metaphor is that of a farmer. What does laboring have to do with being a Christian worker?

8. Why are both human and divine processes necessary for understanding biblical truth (v. 7)?

9. What connections do you see between these three metaphors?

Summary: By these first three metaphors that illustrate the duties of the Christian worker, Paul isolated three aspects of wholeheartedness that should be found in Timothy and in us: the dedication of a good soldier, the law-abiding obedience of a good athlete and the painstaking labor of a good farmer. Without these we cannot expect results. There will be no victory for the soldier unless he gives himself to his soldiering, no wreath for the athlete unless he keeps the rules and no harvest for the farmer unless he toils at his farming.

We come now to a new paragraph before the apostle introduces three more metaphors to illustrate the role of the Christian worker. So far we may summarize his theme by the epigram "nothing that is easy is ever worthwhile," or rather the reverse "nothing that is worthwhile is ever easy." Here Paul continues the same theme.

10. *Read 2 Timothy 2:8-13.* What are the sources of Paul's confidence?

11. How can these verses also give you confidence?

The Christian life is depicted as a life of dying, a life of enduring. Only if we share Christ's death on earth shall we share his life in heaven. Only if we share his sufferings and endure shall we share his reign in the hereafter. For the road to life is death, and the road to glory is suffering.

12. In what specific ways can we die with Christ, endure and remain faithful?

Summary: In verses 1-13 the apostle Paul seemed to have been hammering home a single lesson. From secular analogy (soldiers, athletes, farmers) and from spiritual experience (Christ's, his own, every Christian's) he had been insisting that blessing comes through pain, fruit through toil, life through death and glory through suffering. It is an invariable law of Christian life and service.

So why should we expect things to be easy for us or promise an easy time to others? Neither human wisdom nor divine revelation gives us such an expectation. Why then do we deceive ourselves and others? The truth is the reverse, namely, "no pains, no gains" or "no cross, no crown."

Apply ————————————————————————
■ Compare your motivation with Paul's in verse 10. What do you need to change to follow his example?

What are you doing to pass on the gospel to others?

Pray ─────────────────────────────────

■ What kind of soldier, athlete or farmer are you? Pray that God will help you live out the standards for a Christian worker you have studied.

4
WATCH
YOUR TONGUE

2 Timothy 2:14-26

*T*he word of truth is a target. As we shoot at this target, we will either hit it or miss it.

The word of truth is a road. As we cut this road through the forest, we will make it either straight or crooked.

As a result of our words and teaching, others are bound to be affected, for better or for worse. If we cut the road straight, people will be able to follow and so stay on the way. If, on the other hand, we miss the mark, the attention of the spectators will be distracted from the target and their eyes will follow the arrow however widely astray it has gone.

Of this grave danger Paul warns Timothy here, continuing his vivid portrayal of the role of teachers in transmitting the faith. Paul used three more metaphors—the "workman who does not need to be ashamed," the vessel "for noble purposes" and "the Lord's servant." Each adds a further feature to the portrait. And woven throughout the portrait are instructions for every Christian about our speech.

Open
■ How do your words both contribute to and inhibit the process of getting out the truth about God?

Study

■ *Read 2 Timothy 2:14-19.* Some heretics were substituting for the "word of truth" what Paul called "quarreling about words." The verb he chose referred to something "like the hair-splittings of the schoolmen" in the Middle Ages. In verse 16 he called it "godless chatter" or "empty talk."

1. What various instructions regarding speech are given here?

2. Why is such negative talk such a problem for Christians?

3. The fourth metaphor Paul used to describe the Christian worker is a workman. How do we present ourselves to God as approved workers?

The verb in verse 15 translated "correctly handle" means to "cut straight." The "word of truth" or Scripture is like a freeway that needs to be cut straight through the countryside.

4. How can we handle God's Word correctly?

incorrectly?

5. What sorts of talk would be defined as "godless chatter"?

6. Although the faith of human beings can be upset, the foundation of God remains secure. This is the true church which he is building. It has a twofold "seal" or inscription. Paul's reference is probably from the Old Testament story of the rebellion of Korah, Dathan and Abiram (Numbers 16:5, 26). Both "seals" are essential—the divine and the human. What does this double seal indicate?

Read 2 Timothy 2:20-22. It is doubtless the reference to the necessity of departing from evil that led Paul to the next metaphor, a vessel. The use of the term elsewhere in the New Testament suggests that a vessel stands not simply for members of the church but for the church's teachers. The two sets of vessels in the great house (gold and silver for noble use, wood and earthenware for ignoble) represent true and false teachers in the church. Paul was still referring to the two sets of teachers he contrasted in the previous paragraph, the authentic like Timothy and the bogus like Hymenaeus.

---

7. How can we be vessels for noble use?

It is perfectly true that in his sovereign providence, God has sometimes chosen to use impure vessels as the instruments of both his judgment and his salvation. But these were exceptional cases. The overwhelming emphasis of Scripture is that God chooses to use clean vessels for the fulfillment of his purposes. Certainly, in Paul's exhortation to Timothy he must purify himself if he is to be fit for the Master to use.

---

8. The verb translated "flee" means to "seek safety in flight" or "escape." It is used literally of flight from physical danger and figuratively of flight from spiritual danger. The word for *pursue* is the exact opposite. It means to "run after," "to chase" as in war or hunting. What did Paul tell Timothy to flee and pursue?

---

9. How can these things lead to godly lives?

The metaphor changes yet again. The vessel in the house becomes a slave in the household. But before outlining the kind of behavior fitting to the Lord's servant, Paul set the context in which he had to live and work. He reverted to the worldly debates of verse 14 and the "godless chatter" of verse 16.

---

10. *Read 2 Timothy 2:23-26.* What are some examples of "foolish and stupid arguments" to avoid?

---

11. What qualities should characterize God's servant? Give an example of each.

        Quality   **Example**

Summary: Looking back over the chapter, we are now able to picture in our minds the composite portrait of the ideal Christian minister or worker that Paul painted with a variety of words and images. As good soldiers, law-abiding athletes and hard-working farmers, we must be utterly dedicated to our work. As unashamed workmen, we must be accurate and clear in our exposition. As vessels for noble use, we must be righteous in our character and conduct. And as the Lord's servants, we must be courteous and gentle in our manner.

Thus each metaphor concentrates on a particular characteristic that contributes to the portrait as a whole and, in fact, lays down a condition of usefulness. Only if we give ourselves without reserve to our soldiering, running and farming can we expect results. Only if we cut the truth straight and do not swerve from it shall we be approved by God and have no need to be ashamed. Only if we purify ourselves from what is ignoble, from all sin and error, shall we be vessels for noble use, serviceable to the Master of the house. Only if we are gentle and not quarrelsome, as the Lord's true servants, will God grant our adversaries repentance, knowledge of the truth and deliverance from the devil.

Apply

■ What steps can you take to guard against quarreling and godless chatter?

What do you need to pursue in order to be a more godly worker? Choose something to concentrate on this week.

Pray

■ Ask for God's help to become an approved workman, noble vessel and the Lord's servant as described in this section.

5
LIVING IN
THE LAST DAYS

2 Timothy 3:1-9

As he lay in his cell, a prisoner of the Lord, Paul was still preoccupied with the future of the gospel. His mind dwelled on the evil of the times and Timothy's timidity. Timothy was so weak and the opposition so strong. It seemed absurd that such a man should have been called in such a situation to contend for the truth. So the apostle began with a vivid sketch of the contemporary scene to warn Timothy about what he was up against before summoning him to continue faithful to what he had learned. We face the same opposition today.

Open

■ Describe contemporary people and the present world situation with five adjectives.

Study

1. *Read 2 Timothy 3:1-5.* Why did Paul introduce this section with such an emphatic command to Timothy to "mark this"?

Next, Paul referred to "the last days." It may seem natural to apply this term to a future epoch, to the days immediately preceding the end when Christ returns. But biblical usage will not allow us to do this. For it is the conviction of the New Testament authors that the new age (promised in the Old Testament) arrived with Jesus Christ and that, therefore, with his coming, the old age had begun to pass away and the last days had dawned. This being so, we are living in the last days.

2. Define or explain the attitudes and actions that characterize moral conduct in the last days.

3. Why is "having a form of godliness but denying its power" dangerous?

4. What are some current examples of this religious description?

5. How would you sum up in one sentence the character of those who are described here?

---

6. What did Paul mean by telling Timothy to "have nothing to do with" such people?

Summary: All this unsocial, antisocial behavior—this disobedient, ungrateful, disrespectful, inhuman attitude to parents, together with this absence of restraint, loyalty, prudence and humility—is the inevitable consequence of a godless self-centeredness. The root of the trouble in the last days is that men are "utterly self-centered." Only the gospel offers a radical solution to this problem. For only the gospel promises a new birth or new creation which involves being turned inside out, from self to unself, a real reorientation of mind and conduct, and which makes us fundamentally God-centered instead of self-centered. Then, when God is first and self is last, we love the world God loves and seek to give and serve like him.

---

7. *Read 2 Timothy 3:6-9.* How did Paul describe the actions of these evil people?

---

8. In what kinds of situations are people "always learning but never able to acknowledge the truth" (v. 7)?

As an example of the kinds of false teachers he is describing, Paul mentioned Jannes and Jambres, the names (according to Jewish tradition) of the two chief magicians in Pharaoh's court when Moses sought to lead the Hebrew people out of Egypt (Exodus 7:11). They are not named in the Old Testament text.

9. Why do people like Jannes and Jambres ultimately fail?

Summary: We sometimes get distressed in our day—rightly and understandably—by the false teachers who oppose the truth and trouble the church, especially by the sly and slippery methods of backdoor religious traders. But we need have no fear even if a few weak people may be taken in, even if falsehood becomes fashionable. For there is something patently false about heresy and something self-evidently true about the truth. Error may spread and be popular for a time. But it "will not get very far." In the end it is bound to be exposed, and the truth is sure to be vindicated. This is a clear lesson of church history.

Apply

■ Which of the attitudes and actions cited in these verses do you need to guard against?

How can you do so this week?

Do you know any ungodly people or organizations that you should avoid? If so, what steps will you take to do so?

Pray

■ Ask God to show you any self-centered attitudes in your life. Confess them and pray that God will keep you from entertaining any false teaching that grows out of self-centeredness.

6
BE DIFFERENT

2 Timothy 3:10-17

*E*very Christian is called to be different from the world. "Don't let the world around you squeeze you into its own mold" (Romans 12:2, Phillips). Certainly the pressures on us to conform are colossal, not only from the direct challenge to traditional beliefs and morals but also—and more—from the insidious, pervasive atmosphere of secularism which even seeps into the church. Many give in, often without realizing what they are doing. In stark contrast to the contemporary decline in morals, empty show of religion and spread of false teaching, Timothy—like us—was called to be different and, if necessary, to stand alone.

Open
■ When are you tempted to think and/or act like everyone around you?

Study
1. *Read 2 Timothy 3:10-15.* What key facts about himself does Paul want Timothy to recall?

2. How would Paul's example encourage Timothy at that time?

---

3. Timothy was not to catch the infection of false teaching, nor be carried away by its flood-tide, but to stand out boldly against the prevailing fashion. Why did Paul remind Timothy of what he already knew?

---

4. Why can people who live godly lives expect persecution (v. 12)?

---

5. What were Paul's expectations of Timothy?

---

6. Contrast Timothy's life with the people Paul described in verses 1-9.

Summary: The two reasons Timothy should remain loyal to what he had come firmly to believe were that he had learned it both from Old Testament Scripture and from the apostle Paul. The same two grounds apply today. The gospel we believe is the biblical gospel, the gospel of the Old Testament and the New Testament, vouched for by both the prophets of God and the apostles of Christ. And we must resolve ourselves to heed the exhortation which Paul addressed to Timothy and to abide in what we have learned because of this double authentication.

7. *Read 2 Timothy 3:15-17.* Two fundamental truths about Scripture are asserted here. The first concerns its origin (where it comes from) and the second its purpose (what it is intended for). How would you explain the authority of the Bible from these verses?

The single Greek word literally translated "God-breathed" indicates not that Scripture itself or its human authors were breathed into by God, but that Scripture was breathed or breathed out by God. Scripture is not to be thought of as already in existence when (subsequently) God breathed into it but as itself brought into existence by the breath or Spirit of God. It is clear from many passages that inspiration did not destroy the individuality or the active cooperation of the human writers.

8. What are the purposes of Scripture for our lives?

9. The profit of Scripture relates to both core beliefs and conduct. The false teachers divorced them; we must marry them. How does God's Word accomplish each?

Summary: Christians have responded in different ways to the situation Paul described in the first half of this chapter. Some are swept from their moorings by the floodtide of sin and error. Others go into hiding, as offering the best hope of survival, the only alternative to surrender. But neither of these is the Christian way. "But as for you," Paul says to us as he did to Timothy, "stand firm. Never mind if the pressure to conform is very strong. Never mind if you are young, inexperienced, timid and weak. Never mind if you find yourself alone in your witness. You have followed my teaching so far. Now continue in what you have come to believe. You know the biblical credentials of your faith. Scripture is God-breathed and profitable. Even in the midst of these grievous times in which evil men and impostors go on from bad to worse, it can make you complete and equip you for your work. Let the Word of God make you a man of God! Remain loyal to it and it will lead you on into Christian maturity."

Apply
■ How does this passage encourage you to press on in your beliefs and actions?

On a scale of 1 to 10 (with 10 being the highest), how would you rate your commitment to God's Word?

How can you increase your commitment this week so you live differently from those described in the first part of the chapter?

Pray

■ Ask God to strengthen you in his Word so you are not an easy target for false teaching.

7
NO REGRETS

2 Timothy 4:1-8

*T*his last chapter of 2 Timothy contains some of the very last words the apostle Paul spoke or wrote. He was writing within weeks, perhaps even days, of his martyrdom. For about thirty years without intermission, he labored as an apostle and itinerant evangelist. Truly he had fought a good fight, finished his course and kept the faith. He was awaiting his reward. So these words are Paul's legacy to the church and a challenge to us to live so we won't have any regrets at the end of our lives.

Open
■ If you died today, how would people describe you?

Study
■ *Read 2 Timothy 4:1-5.* The early part of this chapter takes the form of an impressive charge. The verb translated "charge" has legal connections and can mean to "testify under oath" in a court of law or to "adjure" a witness to do so. It is used in the New Testament of any "solemn and emphatic utterance."

1. What key facts does Paul cite about Christ in verse 1?

How does this set the stage for his charge?

2. Why did Paul give Timothy this charge?

3. How was he to carry it out?

4. What would it be like to receive a charge like this?

5. How can we preach the Word as well as correct, rebuke and encourage others?

It has already become apparent that Timothy was timid and that the times in which he lived and worked were—to say the least—dark. He must have recoiled as he read the apostle's solemn charge to him to keep preaching the Word. He would have been tempted to shrink from such a responsibility. So Paul did more than issue a charge; he added incentives.

6. What incentives did Paul give Timothy to preach the Word and fulfill the duties of his ministry (v. 1)?

Why is each important?

Summary: Those difficult days, in which it was hard to gain a hearing for the gospel, were not to discourage Timothy, deter him from his ministry, induce him to trim his message to suit his hearers, or silence him altogether, but to spur him on to preach the more. It should be the same with us. The harder the times and the deafer the people, the clearer and more persuasive our proclamation must be.

7. *Read 2 Timothy 4:6-8.* How appropriate was the epitaph Paul wrote for himself? Why?

Paul used two vivid figures of speech to portray his coming death, one taken from the language of sacrifice and the other (probably) of boats. First, he likened his life to a drink offering. So imminent did he believe his martyrdom to be that he spoke of the sacrifice as having already begun. "Departure" means "loosing" and could be used of untying a boat from its moorings. The two images correspond to some extent, for the end of this life (poured out as a drink) is the beginning of another (putting out to sea).

8. How could Paul maintain this attitude when so many people were turning away from the faith?

9. How would Paul's attitude as he faced death encourage Timothy to endure?

10. Look again at verse 7. In what way would you like to claim the promise of this verse for your life?

Summary: Our God is a God of history. The torch of the gospel is handed down by each generation to the next. As the leaders of the former generation die, it is all the more urgent for those of the next to step forward bravely to take their place. Timothy's heart must have been profoundly moved by this exhortation from Paul, the old warrior who had led him to Christ.

So then, in view of the coming of Christ to judgment, of the contemporary world's distaste for the gospel and of the imprisoned apostle's imminent death, the latter's charge to Timothy had a note of solemn urgency: *Preach the Word!*

Apply ————————————————————————
■ What do you want your epitaph to be?

What can you do this week to begin to make it a reality so you have no regrets when you die?

Pray

■ Talk with God about how you want to be remembered after you die and what changes you will need to make to become that kind of person.

8
STAND FIRM
TO THE END

2 Timothy 4:9-22

F rom his majestic survey of the past and his confident anticipation of the future, Paul returned in thought to the present and his personal predicament. For the great apostle Paul was also a creature of flesh and blood, a man of like nature and passions with ourselves. Although he had finished his course and was awaiting his crown, he was still a frail human being with ordinary human needs. In this last portion of the letter, he described his plight in prison and expressed, in particular, his loneliness.

Open —————————————————————————

■ Describe a time when you felt abandoned by your friends.

Study —————————————————————————

■ *Read 2 Timothy 4:9-22.* Paul did more than issue Timothy an apostolic charge to preach the Word; he gave him an illustration of it from his own example. For he himself had preached the Word, not just throughout his ministry but very recently, bolding proclaiming the gospel in court when on trial for his life before imperial Rome. But now that he was facing death, Paul felt a sense of isolation.

1. What contributed to Paul's loneliness in prison?

2. If you had been in Paul's situation, how would you have felt and/or reacted?

3. Why wasn't Paul bitter about being abandoned by his friends?

4. Demas had been one of Paul's close associates. What do you think are the symptoms of loving this world like Demas did (v. 10)?

5. What can we learn from the people Paul mentioned in this section?

Titus was a close friend who aided Paul in two crises and pastored the church at Crete. Doctor Luke accompanied Paul on his first missionary journey and wrote the books of Acts and Luke. Tychicus was another of Paul's close companions; he carried Paul's letters to the Ephesians, the Colossians and Titus.

Erastus was Corinth's city treasurer whom Paul sent with Timothy into Macedonia. Priscilla and Aquila were "fellow workers in Christ Jesus" with whom he stayed in Corinth. Onesiphorus was Philemon's slave whom Paul had met and led to the Lord when he ran away to Rome. Although Mark had been a deserter on the first missionary journey, later he was restored. Trophimus had been one of Paul's companions during his third missionary journey, and Linus may have been the first bishop of Rome following the martyrdom of Peter and Paul.

---

6. Paul longed for and asked for three things: people, a cloak, and books and parchments. Why were these important to him?

---

7. To admit these needs is not unspiritual; it is human. We must not, then, deny our humanity or frailty or pretend that we are made of other stuff than dust. If you were in Paul's situation, what kinds of things would you long for?

8. How would Paul's attitude toward the circumstances of his first hearing encourage Timothy in his situation?

9. How can we experience the same sufficiency that Paul had in difficult circumstances we face?

Summary: Knowing the sacred deposit entrusted to him, the imminence of his own martyrdom, the natural weaknesses of Timothy, the opposition of the world and the extreme subtlety of Satan, Paul issued to Timothy his fourfold charge regarding the gospel—to guard it (because it is a priceless treasure), to suffer for it (because it is a stumbling block to the proud), to continue in it (because it is the truth of God) and to proclaim it (because it is good news of salvation).

Apply

■ How can Paul's example at the end of his life encourage you when your faith is tested or your friends abandon you?

A new generation of young Timothys is needed, who will guard the sacred deposit of the gospel, who are determined to proclaim it and are prepared to suffer for it, and who will pass it on pure and uncorrupted to the generation which in due course will rise up to follow them.

How can you be faithful to the gospel in your generation?

What is the most important truth you learned from the book of 2 Timothy? Why?

Pray
■ Thank God for what you've learned from this study. Ask him to help you stand firm in your faith when you are tested and to pass on the gospel every opportunity you have.

Guidelines for Leaders

My grace is sufficient for you. (2 Corinthians 12:9)

If leading a Bible study is something new for you, don't worry. These studies are designed to be led easily. As a matter of fact, the flow of questions through the passage from observation to interpretation to application is so natural that you may feel that the studies lead themselves.

You don't need to be an expert on the Bible or a trained teacher to lead a Bible discussion. The idea behind these inductive studies is that the leader guides group members to discover for themselves what the Bible has to say. This method of learning will allow group members to remember much more of what is said than a lecture would.

This study guide is flexible. You can use it with a variety of groups—student, professional, neighborhood or church groups. Each study takes forty-five to sixty minutes in a group setting.

There are some important facts to know about group dynamics and encouraging discussion. The suggestions listed below should enable you to effectively and enjoyably fulfill your role as leader.

Preparing for the Study

1. Ask God to help you understand and apply the passage in your own life. Unless this happens, you will not be prepared to lead others. Pray too for the various members of the group. Ask God to open your hearts to the message of his Word and motivate you to action.

2. Read the introduction to the entire guide to get an overview of the Bible book and the issues which will be explored.

3. As you begin each study, read and reread the assigned Bible passage to familiarize yourself with it.

4. This study guide is based on the New International Version of the Bible. It will help you and the group if you use this translation as the basis for your study and discussion.

5. Carefully work through each question in the study. Spend time in meditation and reflection as you consider how to respond.

6. Write your thoughts and responses in the space provided in the study guide. This will help you to express your understanding of the passage clearly.

7. Get a copy of the Bible Speaks Today commentary by John Stott that supplements the Bible book you are studying. The commentary is divided into short units on each section of Scripture so you can easily read the appropriate material each week. This will help you to answer tough questions about the passage and its context.

It might also help you to have a Bible dictionary handy. Use it to look up any unfamiliar words, names or places. (For additional help on how to study a passage, see chapter five of *Leading Bible Discussions,* InterVarsity Press.)

8. Take the "Apply" portion of each study seriously. Consider how you need to apply the Scripture to your life. Remember that the group will follow your lead in responding to the studies. They will not go any deeper than you do.

Leading the Study

1. Begin the study on time. Open with prayer, asking God to help the group to understand and apply the passage.

2. Be sure that everyone in your group has a study guide. Encourage the group to prepare beforehand for each discussion by reading the introduction to the guide and by working through the questions in the study.

3. At the beginning of your first time together, explain that these studies are meant to be discussions, not lectures. Encourage the members of the group to participate. However, do not put pressure on those who may be hesitant to speak during the first few sessions.

4. Have a group member read the introduction at the beginning of the discussion.

5. Every study begins with an "approach" or "open" question, which is meant to be asked before the passage is read. These questions are designed to connect the opening story with the theme of the study and to encourage group members to begin to open up. Encourage as many members as possible to participate, and be ready to get the discussion going with your own response.

Approach questions can reveal where our thoughts or feelings need to be transformed by Scripture. That is why it is especially important not to read the passage before the approach question is asked. The passage will tend to color the honest reactions people would otherwise give because they are, of course, supposed to think the way the Bible does.

6. Have a group member read aloud the passage to be studied.

7. As you ask the study questions, keep in mind that they are designed to be used just as they are written. You may simply read them aloud. Or you may prefer to express them in your own words.

There may be times when it is appropriate to deviate from the study guide. For example, a question may have already been answered. If so, move on to the next question. Or someone may raise an important question not covered in the guide. Take time to discuss it, but try to keep the group from going off on tangents.

8. Avoid answering your own questions. If necessary, repeat or rephrase them until they are clearly understood. Or point the group to the commentary woven into the guide or perhaps from the Bible Speaks Today commentary to clarify the context or meaning *without answering the question.* An eager group quickly becomes passive and silent if they think the leader will do most of the talking.

9. Don't be afraid of silence. People may need time to think about the question before formulating their answers.

10. Don't be content with just one answer. Ask, "What do the rest of you think?" or "Anything else?" until several people have given answers to the question.

11. Acknowledge all contributions. Try to be affirming whenever possible. Never reject an answer. If it is clearly off-base, ask, "Which verse led you to that conclusion?" or again, "What do the rest of you think?"

12. Don't expect every answer to be addressed to you, even though this will probably happen at first. As group members become more at ease, they will begin to truly interact with each other. This is one sign of healthy discussion.

13. Don't be afraid of controversy. It can be very stimulating. If you don't resolve an issue completely, don't be frustrated. Move on and keep it in mind for later. A subsequent study may solve the problem.

14. Periodically summarize what the group has said about the passage. This helps to draw together the various ideas mentioned and gives continuity to the study. But don't preach.

15. Conclude your time together with the questions under "Apply." Then move into conversational prayer using the suggestions under "Pray" to focus on the themes of the study. Ask for God's help in following through on the commitments you've made.

16. End on time.

Many more suggestions and helps are found in *Small Group Leaders' Handbook* and *The Big Book on Small Groups* (both from InterVarsity Press, US) and *Housegroups* (Crossway Books, UK). Reading through one of these books would be worth your time.

For Further Reading
from InterVarsity Press

The Bible Speaks Today by John Stott
The books in this practical and readable series are companions to the John Stott
Bible Studies. They provide further background and insight into the passages.

The Message of Acts
The Message of Ephesians
The Message of Galatians
The Message of Romans (UK title), *Romans* (US title)
The Message of the Sermon on the Mount (Matthew 5—7)
The Message of 1 & 2 Thessalonians
The Message of 1 Timothy & Titus (UK title), *Guard the Truth* (US title)
The Message of 2 Timothy

4/05